FAITH ERIN HICKS

FRIENDS WITH BOYS

Communities, Culture and Heritage

Faith Erin Hicks recognizes the support of the Province of Nova
Scotia through the Department of Communities, Culture & Heritage.
She is pleased to work in partnership with the Culture Division to
develop and promote our cultural resources for all Nova Scotians.

First Second
New York & London

Text and illustrations copyright © 2012 by Faith Erin Hicks
Published by First Second
First Second is an imprint of Roaring Brook Press, a division of Holtzbrinck Publishing
Holdings Limited Partnership
175 Fifth Avenue, New York, New York 10010

Distributed in the United Kingdom by Macmillan Children's Books,
a division of Pan Macmillan.

Cataloging-in-Publication Data is on file at the Library of Congress

ISBN 978-1-59643-854-5

First Second books are available for special promotions and premiums.
For details, contact: Director of Special Markets, Holtzbrinck Publishers.

First edition 2012
Book design by Colleen AF Venable
Printed in the United States of America

10 9 8 7 6 5 4 3 2 1

FAITH ERIN HICKS
FRIENDS WITH BOYS

:01

First Second
NEW YORK & LONDON

SIGH.

HI DAD.

THIS IS NEW, MAGGIE. YOU'RE UP BEFORE YOUR BROTHERS.

YEAH, WELL, IT'S MY FIRST DAY.

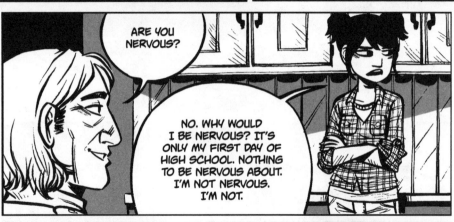

ARE YOU NERVOUS?

NO. WHY WOULD I BE NERVOUS? IT'S ONLY MY FIRST DAY OF HIGH SCHOOL. NOTHING TO BE NERVOUS ABOUT. I'M NOT NERVOUS. I'M NOT.

NERVOUS, THAT IS. I'M NOT NERVOUS.

IT'S OKAY TO BE NERVOUS.

I'M NOT.

SO YOU'VE TOLD ME.

I CAN GIVE YOU A RIDE OVER TO THE SCHOOL IF YOU'D LIKE.

I DON'T THINK IT'D BE A GOOD IDEA FOR ME TO SHOW UP FOR MY FIRST DAY OF HIGH SCHOOL IN A POLICE CAR.

YOU HAVE GOOD INSTINCTS.

IT'S A BIG CHANGE, GOING FROM HOMESCHOOLING TO PUBLIC SCHOOL. I KNOW YOUR BROTHERS WERE NERVOUS WHEN THEY FIRST STARTED.

IT'LL BE WEIRD HAVING A TEACHER WHO ISN'T MOM.

DO WE HAVE ANY CEREAL THAT DIDN'T EXPIRE SIX MONTHS AGO?

IT'S UNLIKELY.

APPARENTLY THE GOOD PEOPLE OF SANDFORD WILL TOLERATE A COP WHO LOOKS LIKE A HIPPIE, BUT A CHIEF OF POLICE IS ANOTHER MATTER.

I'M GETTING MY HAIR CUT ON SATURDAY. WOULD YOU LIKE TO COME WITH ME?

WHAT?? YOU NEVER CUT YOUR HAIR!

THE PROMOTION CAME WITH A MANDATORY HAIRCUT.

BUT... YOU'VE ALWAYS HAD LONG HAIR. YOU'LL LOOK SO DIFFERENT.

IT'S JUST HAIR, MAGGIE.

YEAH, BUT—

THUD

MORNING, DAD.

DANIEL, PLEASE DON'T KILL YOUR BROTHERS BEFORE BREAKFAST.

JUST SHOWING THEM WHO'S REALLY THE OLDEST AROUND HERE.

WHY'S MAGGIE UP BEFORE US?

IT'S MY FIRST DAY OF HIGH SCHOOL.

SO IT IS!

OUR LITTLE BABY SISTER IS ALL GROWN UP AND ENTERING THE REAL WORLD!

DANIEL, DON'T–

I REMEMBER MY FIRST DAY OF GRADE NINE. I WAS SO YOUNG AND INNOCENT.

THE FUTURE LAY BEFORE ME, OPEN TO ENDLESS POSSIBILITIES...

SIIGHH

UM... DANIEL?

THE BEST YEARS OF YOUR LIFE, MAGSBY!

ENJOY THEM BEFORE THEY'RE GONE.

NOW WHAT'S THERE TO EAT AROUND HERE?

A REAL MILESTONE'S BEEN PASSED NOW THAT MAGGIE'S IN HIGH SCHOOL.

YEAH, WHAT?

IT'S EXACTLY SEVENTEEN YEARS SINCE YOUR MOM STARTED HOMESCHOOLING YOU LOT.

YEAH, AND TO CELEBRATE, SHE TOOK OFF.

LATE! YES! WE ARE GOING TO BE LATE FOR SCHOOL IF WE DON'T HURRY AND GO, SO LET US DO THAT RIGHT NOW!

YES. LET US.

BRING YOUR CANE, GRAMPS.

OKAY, YOU'RE DEAD.

DANIEL, WE'LL WALK TO SCHOOL TOGETHER, RIGHT?

NOPE, YOU'RE ON YOUR OWN.

WHAT, WHY?

I DIDN'T HAVE A BROTHER TO WALK TO SCHOOL WITH ON MY FIRST DAY. YOU GOTTA DO IT BY YOURSELF.

A RITE OF *PASSAGE*? SERIOUSLY?

THINK OF IT AS ... *A RITE OF PASSAGE.*

YOU'RE MOVING ON INTO ADULTHOOD, LITTLE MAGSBY.

I GUESS.

SURE YOU DON'T WANT A RIDE?

NO THANKS. IT'S ONLY A TEN MINUTE WALK.

YOU'LL DO FINE, MAGGIE.

THAT'S WHAT EVERYONE KEEPS TELLING ME.

I CAN'T RUN THAT FAST!

hff hff hff

IT'S NOT FAIR! I HATE YOU!

I GOTS A MARS BAR...

HMF!

STUPID GHOST. YOU SCARED ME.

WHAT'RE YOU DOING HERE ANYWAY?

I HAVEN'T SEEN YOU FOR MONTHS.

I WAS KINDA HOPING YOU'D STOPPED STALKING ME.

YES, YOU'RE VERY SPOOKY AND I'M AFRAID.

NOW GO AWAY. I CAN'T BRING A GHOST TO HIGH SCHOOL ON MY FIRST DAY.

I'M SERIOUS! STOP FOLLOWING ME!

HMF.

WILL YOU DO SOMETHING FOR ME?

WISH ME LUCK.

HI-FIVE THMP THMP THMP EEEEE HAHAHA

I... I DON'T WANT TO BE HERE.

HI.

SO. HOW'S THE FIRST DAY GOING?

THERE ARE TOO MANY PEOPLE IN THIS BUILDING, DANIEL.

YEAH, IT'S DIFFERENT FROM A SCHOOL OF FOUR—

IT'S *COMPLETELY* DIFFERENT! I CAN'T DO THIS!

I CAN'T GO TO SCHOOL WITH ALL THESE PEOPLE! DID YOU SEE HOW MANY OF THEM THERE ARE??

IT'S LIKE THOSE COMMUTER TRAINS IN JAPAN!

THEY KEEP PACKING THE PEOPLE IN, AND SOME GUY AT THE BACK GETS CRUSHED TO DEATH. *I COULD DIE!*

THERE'S NO WAY I CAN DO THIS. I CAN'T!

YOU CAN.

I *CAN'T!*

OKAY, WELL THEN, YOU HAVE TO.

MAYBE DAD WOULD LET ME DO HIGH SCHOOL AT HOME—

SO YOU'RE GONG TO STAY HOME YOUR WHOLE LIFE?

WHAT ABOUT GOING AWAY TO COLLEGE? OR TRAVELING? YOU'RE NEVER GOING TO DO ANY OF THAT BECAUSE IT'S AWAY FROM HOME?

NOOO. C'MON, THAT'S NOT FAIR I JUST... IT'S SCARY.

IT'LL GET LESS SCARY.

I PROMISE.

BUT CAN'T THINGS GO BACK TO THE WAY THEY WERE? I LIKED BEING AT HOME.

I KNOW.

YOU LIKED BEING HOMESCHOOLED TOO, DIDN'T YOU?

NO, I LIKE IT HERE BETTER.

REALLY? I DIDN'T KNOW THAT.

YEP. NOW LET'S FIND YOUR CLASS.

BUT WHAT ABOUT MY RITE OF PASSAGE?

THINK OF ME AS YOUR SPIRIT GUIDE.

HI DANIEL!

HEY.

SEE YOU TONIGHT?

ABSOLUTELY.

WHO WAS THAT?

FELLOW DRAMATIC ARTS ENTHUSIAST. DRAMA CLUB MEETS TONIGHT.

DANIEL! HAVE A GOOD SUMMER?

IT WAS KICKASS. AND I HAVE THE BRUISES TO PROVE IT.

SEE YOU TONIGHT?

YOU BET.

ARE YOU *POPULAR?*

NAH, I JUST KNOW A LOT OF PEOPLE.

HERE'S YOUR CLASSROOM.

SEE, NOT SCARY AT ALL.

YOU GOTTA DO THIS, MAGSBY. AND YOU CAN.

SIGH

I'M LUCY, AND THIS IS MY BROTHER ALISTAIR. ARE YOU NEW IN TOWN?

NO, JUST NEW IN HIGH SCHOOL.

HOW'S IT GOING SO FAR?

UM... OKAY, I GUESS.

CITIZENS, LEND ME YOUR EARS!

IN TWO WEEKS, CITIZENS, YOUR BELOVED CHAMPIONSHIP-WINNING VOLLEYBALL TEAM WILL BE PLAYING ITS FIRST GAME OF THE SEASON!

SCHOOL PATRIOTS, I CALL ON YOU TO COME OUT AND CHEER US ON!

WOMEN OF SANFORD HIGH, I ESPECIALLY REQUEST YOUR PRESENCE AT THE GAME.

MATT, COULD YOU BE ANY CHEESIER?

FOR YOU ETHEREAL BEAUTIES, I CERTAINLY COULD BE.

HA HA HA HA HA HA HA HA HA HA

WHATEVER

REMEMBER, TWO WEEKS, CITIZENS! BE A PART OF HISTORY!

SO ARE YOU FRIENDS WITH DANIEL? I SAW YOU WITH HIM BEFORE CLASS—

HE'S MY BROTHER

OH... ARE WE LEAVING?

YEP.

SORRY, GOTTA GO!

NICE MEETING YOU!

FIRST DAY.

HI, ZANDER.

OH HEY. HOW'D THE FIRST DAY GO?

ONLY FREAKED OUT ONCE.

YOU DID BETTER THAN ME.

WHAT'RE YOU DOING?

NOTHING. STARING AT LLOYD.

DANIEL TALKED HIM INTO DOING SET-UP ON THE PLAY THIS YEAR.

ARE YOU GOING TO HELP OUT TOO?

JUST 'CAUSE LLOYD DOES SOMETHING, I GOTTA DO IT TOO?

WHATEVER. LET'S GO.

HEY, ARE YOU AND LLOYD FIGHTING?

WE ALWAYS FIGHT. IT'S OUR THING.

YEAH, BUT IT'S WHEN YOU'RE *NOT* FIGHTING THAT IT'S WEIRD.

WHAT?

I MEAN, BEFORE THIS YEAR YOU GUYS FOUGHT, BUT THEN YOU'D ALWAYS HANG OUT TOGETHER TOO.

NOW *ALL* YOU DO IS FIGHT.

WHY DO I ALWAYS HAVE TO HANG OUT WITH LLOYD?

WELL, BECAUSE—

BECAUSE WE'RE TWINS?

UM, *NO*, BECAUSE YOU *ALWAYS* HANG OUT TOGETHER. OR YOU USED TO.

YEAH, WELL, MAYBE I NEEDED NOT TO BE WITH HIM SOMETIMES.

...OH.

HEY, GOOD FOR YOU. YOU FOUND THE GRADE NINE BATHROOMS.

NOW ALL YOU NEED IS TO FIND YOUR PEOPLE.

IT'S THIS WAY, AL!

YOU COMING?

UM, OKAY.

NEW GIRL FROM SCHOOL, RIGHT?

YEAH, I'M MAGGIE.

I'M USUALLY NOT A STALKER, HONEST. I JUST SAW YOU DOWN THE STREET—

FOUND IT!

I FOUND THE GRAVE, ALISTAIR! I MADE A RUBBING, AND—

—HEY, IT'S MAGGIE.

HOW'D YOU KNOW MY NAME?

YOU'RE DANIEL MCKAY'S SISTER.

AND YOUR DAD'S THE NEW CHIEF OF POLICE. HE HAS LONG HAIR, WHICH IS TOTALLY WEIRD FOR A POLICEPERSON.

I JUST MADE A RUBBING OF A GRAVESTONE I FOUND BACK IN THE OLD SECTION OF THE GRAVEYARD.

I'M PRETTY SURE IT'S THE GRAVE OF A LADY WHOSE HUSBAND DIED AT SEA.

OH... THAT'S SAD.

UH, YEAH. I GUESS IT IS.

EH!

I LOVE GRAVEYARDS. THEY'RE SUCH A GOOD WAY TO GET IN TOUCH WITH HISTORY.

I DON'T KNOW WHY PEOPLE FIND THEM CREEPY.

I THINK PEOPLE MOSTLY OBJECT TO THE DEAD BODIES IN THE GRAVES, LUCY.

BUT THEY'RE DEAD. THEY CAN'T HURT YOU.

THEY CAN IF THEY'RE... *ZOMBIES.*

THAT'S TRUE...

HEY, I USED TO SEE YOUR MOM ALL THE TIME AT THE FARMERS' MARKET.

SHE USED TO HAVE, LIKE, AN ORGANIC COOKIE TABLE AND I'D BUY THE CHOCOLATE CHIP ONES.

I HAVEN'T SEEN HER AT THE MARKET IN FOREVER. THERE'S A NEW GUY SELLING ORGANIC COOKIES, BUT HIS AREN'T AS GOOD.

YOUR MOM SHOULD TOTALLY COME BACK.

WILL YOU TELL HER TO COME BACK?

UM...

I HAVE TO GO.

WHAT JUST HAPPENED?

I DUNNO. HER MOM'S STILL AROUND, ISN'T SHE?

OH GOD!

I THINK I'D LIKE TO CRAWL IN A HOLE AND STAY THERE FOR THE REST OF MY LIFE, OKAY?

OKAY.

THERE YOU ARE. WHERE'D YOU GO?

JUST TO THE GRAVEYARD.

SEE ANY GHOSTS?

THERE'S NO SUCH THING AS GHOSTS.

SO WHAT DO YOU THINK OF THE HAIR?

DO I LOOK LIKE THE CHIEF OF THE EAST COAST'S SMALLEST POLICE FORCE?

YOU ... DON'T REALLY LOOK LIKE *YOU* ANYMORE.

YOU DON'T LIKE IT?

I THOUGHT I LOOKED SORT OF... DASHING.

I DUNNO. IT'S SO DIFFERENT.

NO, IT'S NICE, IT'S JUST...

CHANGE IS GOOD SOMETIMES, KIDDO.

DAD...

WHY DID MOM LEAVE?

YOUR MOM SPENT SEVENTEEN YEARS HOMESCHOOLING YOU GUYS BECAUSE SHE FELT THAT'S WHAT WAS BEST FOR YOU.

DOING SOMETHING LIKE THAT ASKS FOR A LOT OF SACRIFICE.

MAYBE SHE NEEDED TO DO SOMETHING JUST FOR HERSELF, NOT FOR THE FAMILY.

THAT'S NOT A VERY GOOD REASON.

YOUR MOM
LOVES YOU
VERY MUCH,
MAGGIE.

GO AWAY.

ESHERE (AND LLOYD)

PEOPLE SLEEP HERE

SOCCER FIELDS THAT WAY

THE FOOD IS TERRIBLE!

E1

E2

E3

LOCKER BAY

COURT YARD

CAFETERIA

B3

B4

B5

D4 D5 D6 D7

E3

E4 E5 E6

I don't have any classes here

NICE PLACE TO EAT LUNCH

SPORTS?

SOCCER AND TRACK (smelly boys)

E9

Rooms y this ty place llowed !!

LATER—

HI, MAGGIE.

OH, HI.

LUCY SENT ME TO APOLOGIZE.

APOLOGIZE? FOR WHAT?

SHE FEELS BAD ABOUT WHAT SHE SAID IN THE GRAVEYARD. WERE YOU SUPER OFFENDED BY THAT?

OH, GEEZE, NO. OF COURSE NOT.

AWESOME. LUCY KIND OF LIKES YOU AND WOULD REALLY LIKE TO STOP HIDING BEHIND THAT TREE IN SHAME.

AND *I* THOUGHT—

—SINCE YOU'RE EATING LUNCH BY YOURSELF, AND LUCY AND I USUALLY DO THE ALONE THING TOO, THE THREE OF US COULD JOIN UP AND FORM AN AWESOME REBEL SOCIAL GROUP.

WHADDYA SAY?

UMMMM...

SURE, I GUESS SO.

YAY!

72

SHE NEVER GAVE ME AND MY BROTHERS TESTS OR ANYTHING LIKE THAT. SCHOOL WAS MOSTLY WRITING AND LOTS OF READING.

I HAD MY BROTHERS.

BUT WEREN'T YOU LONELY WITHOUT FRIENDS?

IT'D BE *REALLY* AWESOME NOT TO HAVE TESTS. I'M *SO* BAD AT THEM. I GO IN WITH AN A AND COME OUT WITH A C MINUS. IT SUCKS.

IT MUST'VE BEEN WEIRD TO HAVE YOUR MOM FOR A TEACHER—

LUCY...

ARGH, SORRY!

I'M HAVING A FOOT IN MOUTH KINDA DAY. YOU CAN MAKE FUN OF ME IF YOU WANT.

AW, I DON'T WANT TO DO THAT.

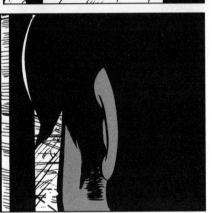

MAGGIE!

HEY...

HEADING HOME?

YEAH.

I'LL WALK WITH YOU.

NO PLAY PRACTICE TODAY?

NOPE. FREE AS A BIRD. THOUGHT I'D SPEND SOME TIME WITH MY FAVORITE SISTER.

I HOPE I DON'T HAVE ANY MORE BROTHERS. THREE IS ENOUGH.

HEY, I LEAVE THE TOILET SEAT DOWN FOR YOU.

I'M YOUR *ONLY* SISTER, DUMMY.

YOU DON'T KNOW THAT. I COULD HAVE OTHER SISTERS.

HOW WELL DO YOU KNOW ALISTAIR?

NOT SUPER WELL. I HAD LUNCH WITH HIM AND HIS SISTER TODAY.

WHAT DO YOU KNOW *ABOUT* HIM?

UM, HE'S IN GRADE 12 AND HAS A MOHAWK?

SHRUG

WHAT DO YOU KNOW ABOUT HIM BEFORE HE HAD THE MOHAWK?

I'VE NEVER SEEN HIM WITHOUT IT.

BEFORE HE SHAVED HALF HIS HEAD, HE WAS SECOND CREEP ON THE LEFT IN THE PACK.

THE WHAT?

SORRY, THAT'S ZANDER'S NICKNAME FOR THE VOLLEYBALL TEAM. MATT AND HIS MERRY BAND OF SOCIAL CONFORMISTS.

ALISTAIR AND HIM HAD SOME FALLING OUT.

IT'S ALL VERY MYSTERIOUS. ONE MINUTE HE AND MATT ARE BROTHERS IN MATCHING WARM-UPS, THE NEXT ALISTAIR'S DECIDED TO STOP DRINKING THE KOOL-AID.

HIS SISTER'S NICE, BUT...

...JUST BE CAREFUL.

SO FAR ALISTAIR AND LUCY ARE THE ONLY PEOPLE WHO TALK TO ME AT SCHOOL.

Y'KNOW, WHAT WITH YOU, LLOYD, AND ZANDER ALREADY HAVING A BILLION FRIENDS.

UNFAIR. I'D EAT LUNCH WITH YOU IF WE HAD THE SAME FREE PERIOD, BUT WE DON'T.

AND I HAVE PLAY PRACTICE AFTER SCHOOL, SO I CAN'T WALK HOME WITH YOU...

YEAH.

WHAT'D ALISTAIR DO TO YOU?

NOTHING IMPORTANT.

JUST THE USUAL HIGH SCHOOL CRAP.

BUT WHY CAN'T YOU—

HEY, LOOK.

POOR ZAN. WONDER HOW FAR HE'LL GET THIS TIME.

SLAM

STOMP STOMP

CRASH
BANG
CLATTER

HOW FAR'D YOU GET THIS TIME, ZANDER?

WOW, THE *POST OFFICE!* A WHOLE *SIX MILES!* IT'S A NEW RECORD!

THE POST OFFICE. OFFICER REYNOLDS BROUGHT ME HOME.

NOT THE FACE.

AAAA

WHAM
POW
CRASH
WHAM

DOING ANYTHING FOR HALLOWEEN?

NOTHING SO FAR. I MISS TRICK OR TREATING. IT WAS SO COOL TO GET PILES OF FREE CANDY.

ALISTAIR WOULD ALWAYS SAVE HIS CANDY, WHICH DROVE ME CRAZY 'CAUSE I'D EAT MINE RIGHT AWAY.

HE'D HAVE PILES OF CANDY FOR MONTHS AFTER HALLOWEEN, AND I WOULDN'T HAVE ANY.

BUT I GOT HIM BACK. I'D SNEAK INTO HIS ROOM AND STEAL IT.

HE NEVER NOTICED.

WHAT'D YOU DRESS UP AS FOR HALLOWEEN?

USUALLY A SUPERHERO OR GHOSTBUSTER. MOM ALWAYS BUGGED ME TO BE A FAIRY PRINCESS OR CINDERELLA, BUT I NEVER WANTED TO BE ANYTHING GIRLY.

ALISTAIR, WHAT D'YOU WANT TO DO FOR HALLOWEEN THIS YEAR?

DUNNO. I'M ASSUMING NEITHER OF YOU ARE SCHOOL DANCE TYPES.

I WAS A PUNK. EVERY YEAR.

ICK, NO.

HEY, I KNOW. WHY DON'T WE GO TO THE OXFORD THEATER?

WHAT'S GOING ON THERE?

THE HALLOWEEN MOVIE MARATHON! MOSTLY IT'S CRAPPY SLASHER FLICKS LIKE "PROM NIGHT," BUT ON WEDNESDAY THEY SHOW "ALIEN."

I *LOVE* "ALIEN." I THINK IT'S MY FAVORITE MOVIE OF ALL TIME.

WAIT... IS "ALIEN" A *SCARY* MOVIE?

CRAZY LINEUP FOR A THIRTY-YEAR-OLD MOVIE.

I READ THINGS ONLINE ABOUT THIS MOVIE AND EVEN READING THEM MADE ME SCARED—

IT'S NOT *THAT* BAD. I WAS TEN WHEN I FIRST SAW IT.

TEN??

YEAH. I SNUCK IN WITH MY BROTHERS.

BOUGHT A TICKET FOR THE LATEST PIXAR MOVIE, THEN MADE LIKE A NINJA FOR THE THEATER SHOWING "ALIEN."

GUYS, I'M SCARED. I DON'T THINK I CAN WATCH THIS MOVIE—

YOU DON'T HAVE TO COME IF YOU DON'T WANT TO, LUCY.

NO, I WANT TO SEE IT.

THIS HASN'T BEEN TOO BAD SO FAR—

CHESTBURSTER

EEEEEE-EEEEAA-AHHHH!

LUCY, THE MOVIE'S OVER.

ALREADY?

IT WASN'T *THAT* SCARY!

THE GIRL WHO KILLED THE ALIEN WAS VERY COOL.

I LIKED HER A LOT.

RIPLEY! YES! ISN'T SHE GREAT? I LOVE HER

SHE LOOKED GREAT IN HER UNDERWEAR TOO.

I RETRACT THE PREVIOUS STATEMENT. I DID NOT LOOK LUSTFULLY UPON THE KICKASS LADY IN HER UNDEROOS.

DAMN STRAIGHT YOU DIDN'T.

THE PART I LIKED BEST WAS THAT RIPLEY DIDN'T FEEL LIKE... OKAY, YOU KNOW THOSE STUPID ACTION MOVIE GIRLS?

"OOHHHH, WHO WILL SAVE LITTLE HELPLESS ME?"

"AH DO DECLARE, I HAVE BEEN RESCUED FROM THE NASTY ALIEN BY A DASHING HERO!

HEAVENS TO BETSY!"

LUCY, I'M GOING TO DROP YOU.

SOME HERO YOU'D BE, AL.

THE FIRST TIME I SAW "ALIEN," I WANTED TO BE RIPLEY.

I REALLY LIKE HER

I MEAN, SHE DRIVES A SPACESHIP AND USES A FLAMETHROWER AND KILLS THE ALIEN IN THE END—

I DUNNO, GROWING UP WITH THREE BROTHERS AND NOT REALLY BEING INTO THE GIRLY STUFF... THERE AREN'T A LOT OF GIRLS LIKE RIPLEY IN MOVIES LIKE "ALIEN."

IT WAS SO COOL TO SEE A GIRL WHO ACTED LIKE A BOY IN AN ACTION MOVIE.

IT'S LIKE SHE WAS IN THE MOVIE JUST FOR ME.

I FELT THE SAME THING WHEN I FIRST HEARD PATTI SMITH'S MUSIC.

LIKE IT WAS MADE JUST FOR ME.

UM... I'M SORRY, BUT WHO'S PATTI SMITH–

OH MY GOD.

OKAY, YOU'RE COMING OVER TO MY HOUSE THIS WEEKEND, AND WE ARE DOING SOME SERIOUS MUSIC SWAPPAGE.

UNDEAD EVIL, PREPARE TO MEET THY DOOM!

WITH THE HELP OF MY FIST!

WHOOSH

YOUR BROTHER'S SO FUNNY.

YEAH, I GUESS.

YOU DON'T THINK HE'S FUNNY?

OH, I DO.

GUESS I'M JUST USED TO HIM.

HEY, WANNA HEAR SOMETHING WEIRD? YOU'RE THE FIRST GIRL I CAN REMEMBER BEING FRIENDS WITH.

YEAH, I THINK SO.

WHAT?? SERIOUSLY??

THAT IS WEIRD.

I'VE ALWAYS HAD MY BROTHERS, SO FOR AGES IT DIDN'T FEEL LIKE I NEEDED ANY OTHER FRIENDS.

PARRY!

LUNGE!

THRUST! HA HA!

I HAD A LOT OF FRIENDS IN MIDDLE SCHOOL, BOYS AND GIRLS.

I LOST TOUCH WITH MOST OF THEM ONCE WE GOT TO HIGH SCHOOL. WHICH IS WEIRD 'CAUSE WE ALL GO TO THIS SCHOOL.

IT'S HARD TO FIND FRIENDS YOU DON'T GROW OUT OF.

DO YOU THINK BEING HOMESCHOOLED KEPT YOU KINDA ISOLATED?

WHAT DO YOU MEAN?

SCHOOL'S ALWAYS BEEN THE MAIN PLACE WHERE I FOUND FRIENDS, 'CAUSE YOU'RE WITH PEOPLE ALL THE TIME. AND IF YOU DON'T HAVE THAT...

...WELL, YOU SAID I WAS THE FIRST GIRL YOU COULD REMEMBER BEING FRIENDS WITH.

HUH. I NEVER THOUGHT OF IT THAT WAY.

YOU HAVE BEEN DEFEATED, VILLAIN!

FWUMP

THIS PLAY HAS EVERYTHING.

HERE COME THE ZOMBIES.

YARG, BRAINS.

YOU AND ALISTAIR SEEM SUPER CLOSE.

I GUESS.

AT LEAST YOU GUYS GET TO HANG OUT TOGETHER.

MY BROTHERS ARE SO BUSY I BARELY SEE THEM.

ALISTAIR'S A JERK.

WORKING HARD?

I'M TOO DISTRACTED BY THE PLAY PRACTICE. IT HAS ZOMBIE SWORDFIGHTS.

SOUNDS LIKE ANOTHER CLASSIC FROM THE STUDENTS OF SANDFORD HIGH.

I'M GOING TO SEE IT *MULTIPLE* TIMES.

LUCY, THIS IS THE LAST WEEK THE MUSEUM'S OPEN, SO IF YOU WANT TO GO, IT'S GOTTA BE NOW.

OOOH!

C'MON, C'MON, WE GOTTA GO!

THEY SHUT IT DOWN AFTER TOURIST SEASON, WHICH SUCKS.

I GUESS I CAN IGNORE THIS ASSIGNMENT FOR A FEW MORE HOURS.

WOOHOO! MARITIME GHOST MUSEUM, HERE WE COME!

WOOHOO! MARITIME GHOST MUSEUM, HERE WE ARE!

MARITIME MUSEUM

NEW EXHIBIT!

TICKETS
ADULT $6.00
CHILD $4.00
FAMILY $12.00

YEAH?

HELLO!
THREE TICKETS
PLEASE.

SERIOUSLY.

*WOOHOO!
MARITIME
GHOST
MUSEUM!
YAY!!!*

YEAH, WHATEVER.
NEXT TOUR'S IN
FIFTEEN MINUTES.

Pirates &
Ghosts of

OKAY, SO, LIKE,
EVERYONE WHO WANTS
TO FOLLOW ME ON A
HAUNTED ADVENTURE OF
SEAFARING... UM, LIKE,
ADVENTURE... UM, FOLLOW
ME, OKAY?

OKAY, SO, LIKE, THIS IS THE "REAPER," A SHIP BUILT FOR THE ROYAL NAVY—

ACTUALLY, IT WAS A SCHOONER DRAFTED INTO PRIVATEERING DURING THE WAR OF 1812.

...UH, YEAH. SO ANYWAY, THE "REAPER" FOUGHT IN LIKE TWELVE BATTLES WITH THE FRENCH—

BRITISH. THEY FOUGHT THE BRITISH.

TRAGEDY at SEA!

...OKAY. SO THEY WERE FIGHTING THE BRITISH THIS ONE TIME IN THE BATTLE OF GHENT—

THERE'S A *TREATY* OF GHENT, BUT NO BATTLE OF GHENT.

IMPRESSIVE, LUCY. I'VE NEVER SEEN SOMEONE'S EYES BUG OUT OF THEIR HEAD LIKE THAT.

I DIDN'T MEAN TO MAKE HER MAD, BUT SHE WAS TELLING IT *WRONG*.

SOME OF THIS STUFF IS *REALLY* CREEPY.

A PIRATE'S FATE

SO WHY DO YOU THINK ALL THIS HAUNTED STUFF IS AWESOME, BUT YOU HATE SCARY MOVIES LIKE "ALIEN"?

DUH! GHOSTS AREN'T SCARY!

... AND NEITHER WAS "ALIEN."

WHAT WAS SO SPOOKY ABOUT THAT SHIP?

THERE WEREN'T ANY GHOSTS IN THE STORY.

LOOK.

Ghostly Legend of the Sea

DO NOT TOUCH!

C'MON!

I'LL SHOW YOU!

IT'S...

THE HAND.

IT'S A RELIC FROM SANDFORD'S SUPERNATURAL PAST!

PROTECTED BY SECURITY'S

THE... WHAT?

C'MON! I'LL SHOW YOU!

AGAIN... THE WHAT?

THIS WAY!

HERE!

IT'S A GRAVE-STONE.

NOT JUST A GRAVESTONE, *THE* GRAVESTONE.

IT'S WHERE THE WIDOW OF THE "REAPER" WAS BURIED.

IT'S *ONLY* SANDFORD'S CREEPIEST GHOST STORY.

IT HAS EVERYTHING! LOVE, DEATH, MYSTERY, PROSTHETIC LIMBS ...EVERYTHING!

THIS ALL HAPPENED BEFORE THE WAR OF 1812, WHEN THE "REAPER" WAS STILL A SCHOONER.

THE "REAPER" WOULD SAIL HERE AND THERE, BRINGING TRADE BETWEEN THE NEW WORLD AND OTHER COUNTRIES.

THE "REAPER" WAS CAPTAINED BY THIS GUY AND HIS THREE SONS, ALL OF WHOM HAD BEEN BORN IN SANDFORD.

SHE WAS THE FASTEST SHIP ON THE WATER.

NO ONE COULD CATCH HER WHEN SHE RAISED HER SAILS.

AND THEN THERE WAS A HUGE TYPHOON, AND THE "REAPER" WAS LOST AT SEA.

NO SIGN OF HER FOR MONTHS AND MONTHS.

BUT THEN, SIX MONTHS AFTER THE "REAPER" WAS ASSUMED LOST, SHE SAILED INTO SANDFORD'S HARBOR.

ANYWAY, ACCORDING TO MY RESEARCH, THIS IS WHERE THEY BURIED THE WIDOW OF THE CAPTAIN OF THE "REAPER."

THE ONLY REMAINS OF NEARLY SEVENTY PEOPLE WHO DISAPPEARED HUNDREDS OF YEARS AGO.

AND THE GHOST MUSEUM SUPPOSEDLY HAS THE PROSTHETIC HAND.

COOL, HUH?

SURE, LUCY. VERY COOL.

THE GRAVEYARD'S *FULL* OF PEOPLE WHO DIED HUNDREDS OF YEARS AGO.

YOU OKAY?

YEAH. I'M FINE.

THE REALLY OLD GRAVESTONES ARE IN THIS SECTION.

HEY, HERE'S A... EUSTICE MCCKAY.

MAYBE YOU'RE RELATED TO HER, MAGGIE.

...BORN 1753, DIED 1806. FIFTY-THREE YEARS OLD!

MAYBE.

THAT STORY DIDN'T FREAK YOU OUT, DID IT?

IT'S FINE. IT WAS INTERESTING.

LUCY FORGETS NOT EVERYONE HAS AN OBSESSION WITH CREEPY OLD LEGENDS. SHE NEVER STOPS TALKING ABOUT THEM.

KINDA DROVE ME CRAZY FOR A WHILE. THE FIRST YEAR SHE WAS IN HIGH SCHOOL, I KEPT PRETENDING SHE WASN'T RELATED TO ME.

BORN 1775, DIED 1789.

WOW, ONLY FOURTEEN YEARS OLD.

I ALWAYS THOUGHT DANIEL SEEMED COOL.

IT SUCKS, THE STUFF MATT AND I PUT HIM THROUGH.

"THE USUAL HIGH SCHOOL CRAP"?

YEAH. DID HE TELL YOU?

NO. SOMEONE ELSE TOLD ME YOU WERE A JERK, BUT YOU SEEM OKAY TO ME.

NAH, THEY'RE RIGHT. I AM A JERK.

WAS THAT BEFORE YOU HAD THE MOHAWK?

OH YEAH, *THAT*.

KIND OF A LONG STORY.

YOU REALLY WANT TO HEAR IT?

YEAH.

MATT'S... GOT THIS GIFT.

HE MAKES YOU FEEL LIKE HE'S THE BEST PERSON IN THE WORLD, AND YOU'RE THAT MUCH BETTER IF YOU'RE HIS FRIEND.

HE'LL EITHER BE A POLITICIAN OR A SUPERVILLAIN WHEN HE GROWS UP.

IT WAS LIKE... *MAGIC.*

AND WE KICKED ASS IN VOLLEYBALL.

WE WERE THE BEST.

AND LUCY WAS ALWAYS THERE, CHEERING ME ON.

...DRIVING ME CRAZY...

MATT DOESN'T HAVE MUCH PATIENCE FOR PEOPLE WHO AREN'T HIS IDEA OF NORMAL.

PEOPLE LIKE DANIEL. Y'KNOW, 'CAUSE HE'S A GUY AND DOES THEATER INSTEAD OF SPORTS.

BITCH.

OR PEOPLE LIKE LUCY, WHO NEED SOMETHING VISUAL TO PROVE THAT THEY'RE DIFFERENT.

ALISTAIR, IF YOUR FREAK SISTER DOESN'T STOP STARING AT US, I'M BENCHING YOU AT THE NEXT GAME.

IT'S EASY TO LOSE YOUR SOUL IN HIGH SCHOOL.

LOOK UP "JERKWAD BROTHER" IN THE DICTIONARY, AND YOU'LL SEE A PICTURE OF ME.

IS THAT WHY YOU SHAVED YOUR HEAD?

OH YEAH, THAT PART.

MATT HAD A PARTY THAT NIGHT. HIS PARENTS BUY HIM BEER IF HE DRINKS AT HOME, SO THAT'S WHERE WE ALL WERE.

ALL I COULD THINK ABOUT WAS LUCY, AND WHAT I'D SAID TO HER.

—HE HAD FRIGGING EYELINER ON. IT MATCHED HIS SOCKS. HE ACTUALLY BOUGHT EYELINER TO MATCH HIS SOCKS.

OH MY GOD. OH MY GOD WHAT A *FREAK*.

YOU SHOULDN'T— YOU SHOULDN'T HAVE SAID THAT.

HOW MANY HAVE YOU HAD, AL? YOU'RE SUCH A LIGHTWEIGHT.

SHE STILL GOES OUT AFTER IT RAINS TO PICK THE WORMS OFF THE SIDEWALK AND PUT THEM BACK IN THE GROUND—

YOU'RE *REALLY* DRUNK!

I'M NOT.

SHE'S JUST... SHE'S... SO SHE'S A LITTLE WEIRD.

YOU SHOULDN'T HAVE SAID SHE WAS A FREAK.

YOU SHOULDN'T HAVE—

I DIDN'T CALL HER ANYTHING. YOU SAID IT TO HER FACE.

WAIT, IS THIS ABOUT YOUR SISTER?

C'MON, MAN. LOOK AT HER AND LOOK AT YOU.

YOU JUST SAID WHAT EVERYONE WAS THINKING.

WSSH

BZZZZZ

Bzzzzzzz

IT WAS ALL I COULD THINK OF TO PROVE TO HER I WAS SORRY.

I QUIT THE VOLLEYBALL TEAM THE NEXT DAY, AND SPENT THE REST OF THE SEMESTER AVOIDING MATT.

HIGH SCHOOL, MAN. IT MAKES YOU CRAZY.

WHAT ABOUT YOU? WHAT'S YOUR BRAND OF CRAZY?

I'M STALKED BY THE GHOST OF A NINETEENTH CENTURY WIDOW.

HAH, YEAH. THAT'S PRETTY CRAZY.

BRAINS!

ALL WE WANT ARE BRAAAINS, BRAAAINS, BRAAAAINS!

BRAINS FOR BREAKFAST, BRAINS FOR LUNCH, SO DELICIOUS WHEN WE CRUNCH CRUNCH CRUNCH THOSE HUMAN BRAAAAAINS!

BRAINS YOU SAY?

BRAINS!

DASTARDLY UNDEAD, YOU SHALL NOT HAVE MY—

BRAINS FOR BREAKFAST, BRAINS FOR LUNCH, WE LOVE THE SOUND OF THEIR CRUNCH CRUNCH CRUNCH—

DANIEL'S REALLY GOOD!

YEAH, HE'S AWESOME.

I NEVER NOTICED HOW CUTE HE IS...

AARRRGHH!

SPURT

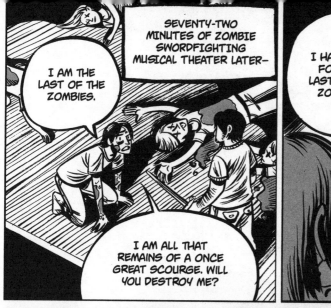

I AM THE LAST OF THE ZOMBIES.

SEVENTY-TWO MINUTES OF ZOMBIE SWORDFIGHTING MUSICAL THEATER LATER—

I HAVE PITY FOR YOU, LAST OF THE ZOMBIES.

I AM ALL THAT REMAINS OF A ONCE GREAT SCOURGE. WILL YOU DESTROY ME?

TAKE MY HAND, AND WE WILL FORGE A NEW WORLD WHERE ZOMBIES AND HUMANS WILL LIVE IN PEACE.

CHOMP

NOOOO! BETRAYED!

HUMANS AND ZOMBIES WILL NEVER BE EQUALS! HUMANS ARE OUR *FOOD!*

BRAINS, BRAINS...

BUT... YOU'RE DEAD...

NOOOOO

NO. WE'RE *UNDEAD.*

CLAP CLAP CLAP CLAP CLAP CLAP

THAT WAS A DEPRESSING ENDING. THE HERO GETS EATEN BY ZOMBIES, WHO THEN GO ON TO RULE OVER THE EARTH?

MAYBE IT'S A METAPHOR.

A METAPHOR FOR WHAT? IT SEEMED LIKE A DEPRESSING ENDING FOR NO REASON. NOW I'M ALL SAD.

DON'T WORRY, IT'S NOT REAL. THE NASTY ZOMBIES DON'T RULE THE WORLD.

THMP THMP THMP THMP

WHAT'D YOU THINK ABOUT THE ENDING, MAGGIE?

DON'T ALL ZOMBIE STORIES HAVE DEPRESSING ENDINGS?

SORRY?

HAH. YOU THOUGHT IT WAS DEPRESSING TOO.

I *GUESS*.

ALL THAT TALK OF BRAIN MUNCHING MAKES ME HUNGRY. WANNA GO GRAB SOME FOOD?

...MOM?

OH!

MAGGIE, I DIDN'T SEE YOU...

LUCY. I HAVE SOMETHING TO TELL YOU.

UM... OKAY.

I'M HAUNTED BY A GHOST.

SHE'S THE WIDOW OF THE CAPTAIN OF THAT SHIP THAT WAS LOST AT SEA. SHE'S HAUNTING ME AND I DON'T KNOW WHY.

WH-WHAT??

WHEN I FIRST STARTED SEEING HER IT WAS ONLY LIKE ONCE A MONTH AND ONLY AT THE GRAVEYARD BUT NOW SHE'S EVERYWHERE I GO AND THEN SHE COMES INTO MY ROOM AND WATCHES ME AND SHE WON'T LEAVE ME ALONE WHAT DOES SHE *WANT*?

UM... I... SOMETIMES GHOSTS HAVE UNFINISHED BUSINESS ON EARTH... MAYBE SHE WANTS YOU TO DO SOMETHING FOR HER.

IF I DO WHAT SHE WANTS, WILL SHE LEAVE ME ALONE? WILL THINGS GO BACK TO NORMAL?

I DON'T KNOW. WHAT'S NORMAL?

SOMETHING... NOT *THIS*. NOT THE WAY THINGS ARE NOW.

WHAT ABOUT THE HAND OF THE CAPTAIN OF THE "REAPER"?

THAT YOU SHOWED ME AT THE MUSEUM?

YOU SAID THE HAND WAS THE ONLY THING LEFT AFTER THE CREW OF THE "REAPER" DISAPPEARED.

MAYBE IF WE BROUGHT THE HAND TO THE GHOST, SHE'D BE REMINDED TO JOIN HER FAMILY IN THE AFTERLIFE.

UM... MAYBE...

WE SHOULD DO THAT. WE SHOULD BORROW THE HAND FROM THE MUSEUM AND SHOW IT TO THE GHOST.

WILL YOU HELP ME?

WILL I... DO YOU THINK I'D GET TO SEE THE GHOST?

YEAH. I PROMISE.

COME OVER TO MY PLACE TONIGHT. WE'LL DO A SLEEPOVER.

THEN WE'LL SNEAK INTO THE MUSEUM AFTER DARK AND BORROW THE HAND.

WE'LL RETURN IT AFTERWARDS. NO ONE WILL EVER KNOW.

HEY.

HI.

MAGGIE AND I ARE GOING TO TRY AND SEE A GHOST TONIGHT.

YEAH, SHE TOLD ME SHE SEES GHOSTS.

NOT GHOSTS. *ONE* GHOST.

YOU WANT TO COME WITH US?

NAH. I GOT HOMEWORK.

POW!

SCREW IT.

MARITIME MUSEUM

NEW EXHIBIT!

THIS LOOKS UNLOCKED.

CREAK

JEEZE, THEY'RE NOT MUCH FOR SECURITY.

Pirate Weapons

HELLO.

NOK NOK

UM, HI. IS LUCY HERE?

NO, SHE AND MAGGIE WENT OUT.

I THINK THEY WENT TO TRY AND SEE A GHOST? I DUNNO. TRY THE GRAVEYARD.

THANKS.

HEY... UM...

I'VE BEEN MEANING TO TALK TO YOU A WHILE, LUCY.

ABOUT WHAT, MATT?

I WAS JUST WONDERING HOW ALISTAIR WAS DOING...

HE'S FINE.

REALLY.

I CAN'T FIGURE OUT WHAT HAPPENED WITH AL.

I'D REALLY LIKE TO KNOW WHY MY FORMER BEST FRIEND WOULD RATHER HANG OUT WITH FREAKS THAN WITH ME.

I DON'T KNOW, MATT. WHY DON'T YOU ASK HIM?

BECAUSE HE WON'T TALK TO ME ANYMORE.

LEAVE US ALONE, MATT.

HUH.

WONDER WHERE THEY ARE.

CRUD.

LOOK, LUCY—

MY DAD'S A COP.

HE'S REALLY TALL. AND HAS, LIKE, A GUN.

I KNOW YOU. YOU'RE THE FOURTH MCKAY.

HEY!

LUCY, LET'S GO.

YOU'RE *LEAVING*?

C'MON, DON'T LEAVE.

WHAT'S THAT?

DON'T–

MATT, DON'T BE A JERK.

DON'T BE A *JERK*?

YEAH. DON'T BE A *JERK*.

COME *ON,* MATT.

Y'KNOW, WE HAVE A CHOICE HOW WE'RE GOING TO ACT IN HIGH SCHOOL.

I DON'T *WANT* TO BE THAT GUY BEING AN ASSHOLE TO THAT OTHER GUY JUST BECAUSE HE DOES THEATER INSTEAD OF SPORTS, OKAY? THAT CRAP STAYS FOR LIFE, WHETHER WE WANT IT TO OR NOT.

I'M TIRED OF BEING THAT ASSHOLE, MAN.

SO I DON'T WANT TO BE YOUR FRIEND.

NO—

I HOPE YOU DIE, YOU JERKS!

I HOPE YOU DIE!

ALISTAIR?

HEY...

HI.

Y'KNOW... I THINK I HURT HIS FEELINGS.

HOW WEIRD IS THAT?

MAGGIE...

SOMEONE BROKE INTO THE MUSEUM AND STOLE SOMETHING.

DO YOU KNOW WHAT?

A NINETEENTH CENTURY PROSTHETIC HAND.

EXACTLY.

I NEED TO KNOW WHAT HAPPENED.

I NEED YOU TO KNOW WHAT YOU AND THOSE OTHER TWO KIDS WERE DOING OUTSIDE THE MUSEUM AT ELEVEN O' CLOCK AT NIGHT.

MAGGIE...

...IF THIS IS A SITUATION YOU FEEL LIKE...YOU WERE FORCED TO TAKE PART...

IF YOU FEEL LIKE YOU *HAD* TO GO ALONG WITH THESE TWO KIDS...

NO.

I STOLE THE HAND FROM THE MUSEUM. NOT ALISTAIR AND LUCY.

GO GET IN THE CAR, MAGGIE.

BUT—

NOW.

DAD—

GO INSIDE.

DAD, WHAT'LL HAPPEN TO LUCY AND ALISTAIR?

THAT'S NONE OF YOUR BUSINESS.

I WANT TO KNOW!

THERE'LL BE AN INVESTIGATION. WE WILL TRY TO RECOVER THE MUSEUM'S PROPERTY.

NOW GO INSIDE.

I STOLE THE HAND FROM THE MUSEUM..

IT WAS ME. NOT THEM.

THE ONLY REASON YOU'RE NOT BACK AT THE STATION WITH THOSE TWO IS BECAUSE YOU'RE MY KID.

GO UPSTAIRS. YOU'RE GROUNDED FOR THE REST OF THE SEMESTER. NOTHING BUT SCHOOL AND HOMEWORK, UNDERSTAND?

JEBUS, MAGGIE. USE YOUR WORDS.

I'M A BAD DAUGHTER.

I THINK THAT'S WHY MOM LEFT.

DAD ALWAYS HAD YOU, LLOYD, AND ZANDER AND MOM SHOULD'VE HAD ME, BECAUSE I WAS A GIRL.

BUT I NEVER WANTED TO BE WITH HER, BECAUSE SHE ONLY WANTED TO DO GIRL THINGS.

I WANTED TO BE WITH YOU AND LLOYD AND ZANDER AND DAD AND DO BOY THINGS.

DO YOU REMEMBER WHEN WE WENT TO SEE "ALIEN" LAST YEAR?

YEAH.

SHE'D PLANNED A SHOPPING TRIP THE TWO OF US. SHE SAID IT WAS A TRIP "JUST FOR THE GIRLS."

BUT I DIDN'T WANT TO GO SHOPPING. SHOPPING WAS A STUPID GIRLY THING. I WANTED TO GO SEE "ALIEN" WITH YOU GUYS.

AND WE HAD THIS HUGE FIGHT AND SHE ASKED ME WHY I NEVER WANTED TO BE WITH HER

AND I TOLD HER IT WAS BECAUSE I LIKED BEING WITH MY BROTHERS AND DAD BETTER THAN BEING WITH HER

DID DAD TELL YOU WHAT HAPPENED TONIGHT?

HE SAID SOMETHING WAS STOLEN FROM THE MUSEUM.

I STOLE THE PROSTHETIC HAND OF A SAILOR WHO WAS LOST AT SEA IN THE NINETEENTH CENTURY.

THEN MATT AND THE PACK STOLE IT FROM ME.

I DON'T KNOW WHAT TO DO.

I CAN STEAL THE HAND BACK AND RETURN IT TO THE MUSEUM.

I...KNOW WHERE THE PACK'S EVIL LAIR IS.

ORRRR... WE COULD TELL OUR LAW ENFORCEMENT FATHER AND HE COULD DEAL WITH IT.

DAD MADE SURE I WASN'T ARRESTED FOR STEALING THE HAND, EVEN THOUGH I DID. HE COULD LOSE HIS JOB.

I'M NOT GOING TO AN EVIL LAIR WITHOUT NINJA BACKUP.

WOW, I DIDN'T KNOW YOU COULD DO THAT.

THERE'S LOTS ABOUT ME YOU DON'T KNOW.

YEAH, LIKE HOW YOU'VE TURNED TO A LIFE OF CRIME?

OKAY, FINE. I STOLE SOMETHING FROM THE MUSEUM DOWNTOWN, AND THEN THE PACK STOLE IT FROM ME.

DANIEL AND I NEED YOUR HELP TO STEAL IT BACK.

WHAT?? NO *WAY!* I'M NOT GOING UP AGAINST *THEM!*

ME NEITHER! I WANT TO *SURVIVE* HIGH SCHOOL!

THAT'S THE FIRST TIME YOU GUYS HAVE AGREED ON SOMETHING IN ABOUT A MILLION YEARS.

IS IT THE TWIN THING?

THE TWIN THING?

...YEAH.

WH—WHAT?

I CAN'T DO ANYTHING WITHOUT PEOPLE ASKING WHERE YOU ARE.

THEY THINK WE DON'T EXIST AS SEPARATE PEOPLE! LIKE WE'RE ONE BRAIN IN TWO BODIES.

IT'S SO INSULTING.

JUST BECAUSE WE'RE TWINS.

I MISS YOU, MAN. I WISH YOU'D GET OVER YOURSELF AND COME HANG WITH ME. SCREW THE STEREOTYPES.

I...I MISS YOU TOO, MAN.

YOU'RE MY BEST FRIEND, MAN!

YOU'RE MY BEST FRIEND TOO, MAN!

OKAY, FOR REAL, ARE WE DOING THIS OR NOT?

C'MON.

MOVE.

THIS IS A JOB FOR SOMEONE WHO'S SEEN "RAIDERS OF THE LOST ARK" THREE HUNDRED AND FOURTEEN TIMES.

HEY!

WHO WAS THAT?

HAHAHAHA!

THEME SONG TIME! DUN DAH DUN DUN, DUN DA DUNNNNN!

DUN DA DUN DAAA DUN DA DUNN DAH DAHHHH!

AND I WAS ALL, "YEAH! I'M GONNA *TAKE THAT*-"

HEY, WHERE'D MAGGIE GO?

SHE'S NOT BEHIND US?

SHE WAS A MINUTE AGO.

I HAVE WHAT YOU WANT.

YOU CAN GO HOME TO YOUR HUSBAND AND YOUR SONS NOW.

HERE! TAKE IT AND GO HOME!

WHAT'S WRONG WITH YOU? DON'T YOU WANT TO BE WITH YOUR FAMILY?

DON'T YOU KNOW HOW MUCH THEY MISS YOU?

MAGGIE...

CAN YOU...ARE YOU TALKING TO... THE GHOST?

YOU CAN SEE IT TOO?

WELL, YEAH. IT'S RIGHT THERE.

BUT...NOBODY ELSE HAS BEEN ABLE TO SEE IT BEFORE.

I'VE ALWAYS SEEN IT. EVER SINCE I WAS A KID.

WHY DIDN'T YOU TELL ME?

...WELL, GEEZE.

I ONLY WEAR THIS SHIRT, LIKE, EVERY DAY.

MAGGIE, WHAT'S GOING ON WITH YOU?

I DON'T KNOW. I WANTED TO FIX THINGS FOR HER, FINISH HER UNFINISHED BUSINESS.

I THOUGHT IT WAS SOMETHING I *COULD* FIX.

BUT I CAN'T FIX ANYTHING.

MAYBE THAT'S OKAY.

SOMETIMES IT'S NOT.

YEAH, I KNOW.

YEAH, CALL THE PARENTS AND TELL THEM THE MATTER'S BEEN RESOLVED. THANK YOU. BYE.

CLICK

GET TO
SCHOOL,
YOU LOT.

STOP IT.

NO, SERIOUSLY, IF YOU JUST PUT THE BUNS ON THE SIDE, YOU COULD PULL OFF A PRINCESS LEIA.

I DON'T GET WHY PEOPLE DON'T LIKE THE LEIA HAIR.

IT COMBINES TWO OF THE GREATEST THINGS IN THE WORLD: SCIENCE FICTION AND BREAKFAST PASTRIES.

STOP IT.

BETTER STOP, LLOYD.

BUT I'M GETTING IN TOUCH WITH MY INNER HAIRDRESSER...

OH, HERE THEY COME.

WAIT. CAN YOU—

DO YOU MIND WAITING WITH ME?

SURE.

NO PROBLEM.

UM, HI.

DID SOMEONE FROM THE POLICE STATION CALL YOUR PARENTS?

YEAH.

THE POLICE SAID THE THING WE SUPPOSEDLY STOLE WAS RETURNED TO THE MUSEUM.

SO OBVIOUSLY WE DIDN'T STEAL IT.

I'M REALLY SORRY ABOUT WHAT HAPPENED.

ME TOO.

I DIDN'T GET TO SEE A GHOST.

YEAH, I GUESS
THEY'RE SHY
THIS TIME OF
YEAR.

HI.

HI.

UM...THESE
ARE MY BROTHERS.
LLOYD, ZANDER,
AND DANIEL.

HI.

YOU WERE GREAT IN THE PLAY.

I COMPLETELY BELIEVED YOU WERE HORRIBLY KILLED BY ZOMBIES.

THANKS. IT'S A GIFT.

RRRIINNG

OH, FIRST BELL.

COMING?

YEAH.

EARLY SKETCHES

LUNCH OUTFIT
↙ no necklace

Movie Outfit

↙ short sleeves

ACKNOWLEDGMENTS

All of the following people played a part in the creation of *Friends with Boys*, so I owe them several fruit baskets as well as thanks. Thanks to the amazing First Second ninja squad: Calista Brill, Colleen AF Venable, Gina Gagliano, and Mark Siegel; my awesome agent Bernadette Baker-Baughman; Shelly Bond; Tim Larade; and my family: Mom, Dad, Noah, Nathan, and Eli.